WHERE FOOD COMES FROM

BEE TO HONEY

Sarah Ridley

CRABTREE
PUBLISHING COMPANY
WWW.CRABTREEBOOKS.COM

Published in Canada
Crabtree Publishing
616 Welland Avenue
St. Catharines, ON
L2M 5V6

Published in the United States
Crabtree Publishing
PMB 59051
350 Fifth Ave, 59th Floor
New York, NY 10118

Published in 2019 by Crabtree Publishing Company

First Published in Great Britain in 2018 by Wayland
Copyright © Hodder and Stoughton, 2018

Author: Sarah Ridley

Editors: Sarah Peutrill, Petrice Custance

Design: Matt Lilly

Proofreader: Ellen Rodger

Prepress technician: Margaret Amy Salter

Print coordinator: Katharine Berti

Printed in the U.S.A./082018/CG20180601

Thank you to Colchester beekeeper, Alan Hayden-Case, for his help with this book.

Photographs

arlindo71/Istockphoto: front cover t, 1t,9. temmuz can arsiray/Istockphoto: 2, 17, 19, 24l. BirdofPrey/Istockphoto: 18. Marc Bruxelle/Istockphoto: 20tr. Scott Camazine/Alamy: 14. Simon Colmer/Nature PL: 11. Dragisa/Istockphoto: 16. Gregory Dubus/Istockphoto: 20bl. Tom Gowanlock/Shutterstock: 3cr. Imo/Istockphoto: 23tr. Kaanates/Istockphoto: 23tc. T. Kimura/istockphgoto: 23br. Evan Lorne/Shutterstock:. 21tr Nattika/Shutterstock: 23cr. Stefa Nikolic/Istockphoto: 4, 5. Olgysha/Shutterstock: 22. Photogal/Shutterstock: 23bl. Photografiero/Istockphoto: 8. Photografiero/Shutterstock: 10. Proxyminder/Istockphoto: 6b, 12. Real444/Istockphoto: 23cl. sumikophoto/Shutterstock: 15. Sergey Sushitsky/Shutterstock: 13. Tienduong/Dreamstime: 7cl, 7tr, 24tr. Samo Trebizan/Shutterstock: 3bl. Tim UR/Shutterstock: 23tl. Valentyn Volkov/Shutterstock: 1b, 3tl, 21l. John Williams RUS/Shutterstock: 6t. Slawomir Zelasko/shutterstock: front cover b.

Library and Archives Canada Cataloguing in Publication

Ridley, Sarah, 1963-, author
     Bee to honey / Sarah Ridley.

(Where food comes from)
Includes index.
Issued in print and electronic formats.
ISBN 978-0-7787-5119-9 (hardcover).--
ISBN 978-0-7787-5130-4 (softcover).--
ISBN 978-1-4271-2167-7 (HTML)

     1. Honey--Juvenile literature. 2. Honeybee--Juvenile literature.
3. Bee culture--Juvenile literature. I. Title.

SF539.R53 2018   j638'.16   C2018-902471-2
                                          C2018-902472-0

Library of Congress Cataloging-in-Publication Data

CIP available at the Library of Congress

CONTENTS

HONEY

HONEYCOMB

Honey is a sweet, sticky food. We eat it in yogurt, on bread, and many other different ways.

But where does honey come from?

BUSY BEES

Honey is made by honeybees. People who raise bees for honey are called beekeepers. They keep bees in containers called hives. Beekeepers can own one or many hives.

A hive has several layers. When a beekeeper checks a hive, he or she wears special clothes to protect themselves from bee stings.

HIVE

BEES

As the air warms up in the morning, some of the honeybees start to leave their hive to look for food.

The bees fly from flower to flower searching for **nectar**.

This bee can smell the nectar inside the purple flower.

She sucks up the nectar into her honey stomach.

BEE FACT

Bees have two stomachs. One is for regular eating. The other, known as a honey stomach, is where a bee stores nectar to bring back to the hive.

7

Another honeybee visits some **blossoms**. As well as nectar, she collects pollen, cramming it into pollen baskets on her back legs.

WONDER WORD:
POLLEN

Pollen is a powder made by the male part of a flower called the **stamen**. Bees feed pollen to their young.

8

Honeybees are about one-half inch (15 mm) long.
Here are some of the different parts of a honeybee:

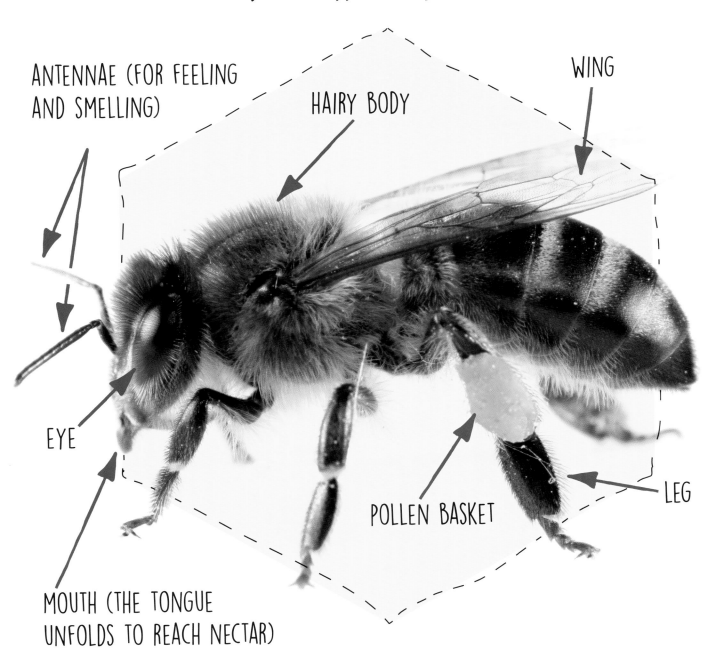

ANTENNAE (FOR FEELING AND SMELLING)

HAIRY BODY

WING

EYE

MOUTH (THE TONGUE UNFOLDS TO REACH NECTAR)

POLLEN BASKET

LEG

INSIDE THE HIVE

The bees collect more and more nectar until it is time to fly back to the hive to unload.

BEE FACT

A honeybee visits between 50 and 100 flowers on each trip.

Inside the hive, the bees pass the nectar from one bee to another, slowly turning it into honey.

BEE FACT

During the summer, honeybees feed on nectar and a little pollen.

Honeybees build wax cells in flat frames inside the hive. A cell is like a little box for storing honey. A hive contains several frames.

Honeybees stick many wax cells together to build a **honeycomb** to store the honey. The bees fan the honey with their wings to remove any water and make the honey thick.

WAX LID

HONEY IN CELL

When the honey is ready, bees seal the cells with a wax lid. Bees feed on honey during the winter months.

Before bees set off to collect nectar, a bee that has already collected some starts to dance!

This dance tells the bees where to find flowers full of nectar.

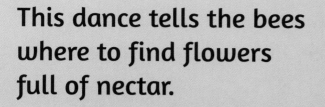

This bee has set off to collect nectar. She will make about ten trips back to the hive before the end of the day.

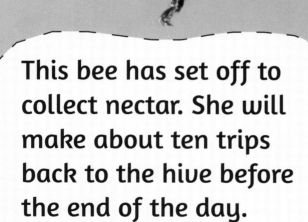

BEE FACT

HONEY

In her lifetime of about 40 days, a honeybee will collect enough nectar to make about one-twelfth of a teaspoon of honey.

15

All the bees in one hive are called a **colony**. The queen bee controls the colony and lays eggs, which hatch into larvae.

QUEEN BEE

WONDER WORD:
LARVAE

Many insects, **amphibians**, and fish lay eggs that hatch into young called larvae.

Worker bees feed plant pollen to the growing larvae in their wax cells. After a few weeks, the larvae become young bees.

LARVAE

BEE FACT

In the summer, a colony can grow to about 50,000 bees.

COLLECTING THE HONEY

During the summer, honeybees usually make so much honey that beekeepers can collect some. To keep the bees calm while the hive is open, beekeepers puff smoke from a smoker into the hive.

SMOKER

This frame of honeycomb is full of honey. The beekeeper will take it home to **extract** the honey.

First, the beekeeper uses a tool to scrape off the wax lids made by the bees.

Then the beekeeper puts the honeycomb frames into a spinner. Spinning the honeycomb makes the honey run out.

The honey flows out of the spinner and through a **sieve** to catch any bits of wax.

Sometimes honey is heated to keep it runny. The beekeeper pours the honey into jars and the honey is ready to eat!

BEE FACT

Honeybees must collect nectar from about two million flowers to make one 16 oz (454 g) jar of honey.

THE IMPORTANCE OF BEES

As well as making honey, bees help plants make seeds and fruit. While collecting nectar and pollen, pollen grains get stuck to a bee's hairy body.

Some of this pollen brushes off on the female parts of the next flower the bee visits. This is called pollination.

STRAWBERRIES

ALMONDS

KIWI FRUIT

APPLE

All sorts of plants are pollinated by bees and other insects. Many of these plants grow the fruits and vegetables that we like to eat.

Without bees, less plants would grow, and we could face a shortage of food.

NECTARINE

RUNNER BEANS

WONDER WORD:
POLLINATION

Pollination takes place when the male part (pollen) of one flower reaches the female part of another, allowing it to make seeds or fruit.

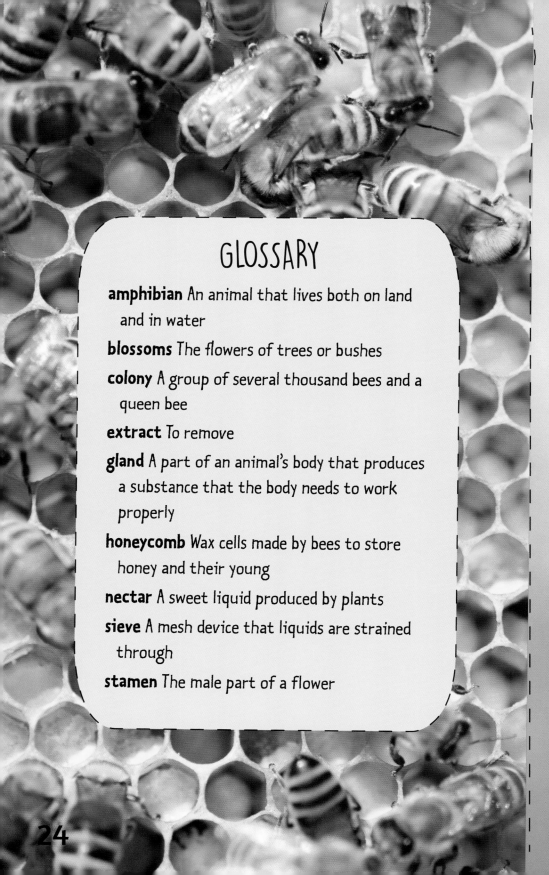

GLOSSARY

amphibian An animal that lives both on land and in water

blossoms The flowers of trees or bushes

colony A group of several thousand bees and a queen bee

extract To remove

gland A part of an animal's body that produces a substance that the body needs to work properly

honeycomb Wax cells made by bees to store honey and their young

nectar A sweet liquid produced by plants

sieve A mesh device that liquids are strained through

stamen The male part of a flower

INDEX

24